TRAVEL JOURNAL

First published in 2019 by Erin Rose Publishing

Text and illustration copyright © 2019 Erin Rose Publishing

Design: Julie Anson

THIS TRAVEL JOURNAL BELONGS TO:

....

AGE: ....

My Adventure To: ....

MY JOURNEY STARTS AT: ....

AND ENDS IN: ....

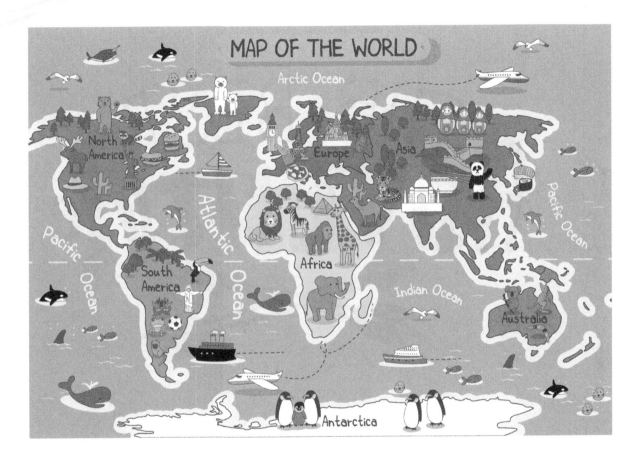

JANUARY	FEBRUARY	MARCH	APRIL	MAY	JUNE	JULY	AUGUST	SEPTEMBER	OCTOBER	NOVEMBER	DECEMBER

THE BEST ADVENTURE

HOW LONG IS THE JOURNEY? ....

HOW AM I TRAVELLING? ....

WHERE AM I STAYING? ....

WHO IS GOING? ....

WHAT WOULD I LIKE TO DO WHEN I GET THERE? ....

....

....

....

....

....

WHAT AM I MOST LOOKING FORWARD TO? ....

....

....

....

WHAT DO I NEED TO PACK? YOU CAN WRITE YOUR PACKING LIST BELOW:

....

....

....

....

....

....

....

....

....

....

....

DATE:........................ LOCATION:.. TODAY'S STAR RATING: ☆☆☆☆☆

TRAVELLED BY: ✈ PLANE ☐ 🚢 BOAT ☐ 🛣 ROAD ☐ 🪧 WALK ☐ 🎈 OTHER ☐

WHERE DID I VISIT?

WHO WAS THERE?

WHAT I DISCOVERED?

WHO DID I MEET?

MY FAVOURITE THING WAS:

MY MOOD WAS 😄 ☐ 🙂 ☐ 😐 ☐ 🙁 ☐ 😎 ☐ 😴 ☐

WEATHER ☀ ☐ ⛅ ☐ 🌦 ☐ ⛈ ☐ 🌧 ☐ 🌨 ☐

PICTURE OF THE DAY

DRAW, SKETCH OR STICK-IN A PICTURE OR KEEPSAKE OF YOUR DAY.

DATE:..................... LOCATION:................................... TODAY'S STAR RATING: ☆ ☆ ☆ ☆ ☆

TRAVELLED BY: ✈ ☐ 🚢 ☐ 🛣 ☐ 🪧 ☐ 🎈 ☐
PLANE   BOAT   ROAD   WALK   OTHER

WHERE DID I VISIT?

WHO WAS THERE?

WHAT I DISCOVERED?

WHO DID I MEET?

MY FAVOURITE THING WAS:

MY MOOD WAS 😄 ☐ 🙂 ☐ 😐 ☐ ☹ ☐ 😎 ☐ 😴 ☐

WEATHER ☀ ☐ ⛅ ☐ 🌦 ☐ ⛈ ☐ 🌧 ☐ 🌨 ☐

PICTURE OF THE DAY

DRAW, SKETCH OR STICK-IN A PICTURE OR KEEPSAKE OF YOUR DAY.

DATE:........................... LOCATION:... TODAY'S STAR RATING: ☆☆☆☆☆

TRAVELLED BY: ✈ PLANE ☐   🚢 BOAT ☐   ROAD ☐   🪧 WALK ☐   🎈 OTHER ☐

WHERE DID I VISIT?

WHO WAS THERE?

WHAT I DISCOVERED?

WHO DID I MEET?

MY FAVOURITE THING WAS:

MY MOOD WAS 😄 ☐ 🙂 ☐ 😐 ☐ 🙁 ☐ 😎 ☐ 😴 ☐

WEATHER ☀ ☐ ⛅ ☐ 🌦 ☐ ⛈ ☐ 🌧 ☐ 🌨 ☐

PICTURE OF THE DAY

DRAW, SKETCH OR STICK-IN A PICTURE OR KEEPSAKE OF YOUR DAY.

DATE:.......................... LOCATION:....................................... TODAY'S STAR RATING: ☆☆☆☆☆

TRAVELLED BY: ✈ PLANE □ 🚢 BOAT □ 🚗 ROAD □ 🪧 WALK □ 🎈 OTHER □

WHERE DID I VISIT?

WHO WAS THERE?

WHAT I DISCOVERED?

WHO DID I MEET?

MY FAVOURITE THING WAS:

MY MOOD WAS 😄 □ 🙂 □ 😐 □ 🙁 □ 😎 □ 😴 □

WEATHER ☀ □ ⛅ □ 🌦 □ ⛈ □ 🌧 □ 🌨 □

PICTURE OF THE DAY

DRAW, SKETCH OR STICK-IN A PICTURE OR KEEPSAKE OF YOUR DAY.

DATE:........................ LOCATION:.. TODAY'S STAR RATING: ☆☆☆☆☆

TRAVELLED BY: ✈ □ 🚢 □ 🛣 □ 🪧 □ 🎈 □
               PLANE   BOAT   ROAD   WALK   OTHER

WHERE DID I VISIT?

WHO WAS THERE?

WHAT I DISCOVERED?

WHO DID I MEET?

MY FAVOURITE THING WAS:

MY MOOD WAS 😄 □ 🙂 □ 😐 □ 🙁 □ 😎 □ 😴 □

WEATHER ☀ □ ⛅ □ 🌦 □ ⛈ □ 🌧 □ 🌨 □

PICTURE OF THE DAY

DRAW, SKETCH OR STICK-IN A PICTURE OR KEEPSAKE OF YOUR DAY.

DATE:........................ LOCATION:... TODAY'S STAR RATING: ☆☆☆☆☆

TRAVELLED BY: ✈ ☐ PLANE 🚢 ☐ BOAT 🌄 ☐ ROAD 🪧 ☐ WALK 🎈 ☐ OTHER

WHERE DID I VISIT?

WHO WAS THERE?

WHAT I DISCOVERED?

WHO DID I MEET?

MY FAVOURITE THING WAS:

MY MOOD WAS 😄 ☐ 🙂 ☐ 😐 ☐ 🙁 ☐ 😎 ☐ 😴 ☐

WEATHER ☀ ☐ ⛅ ☐ 🌦 ☐ ⛈ ☐ 🌧 ☐ ❄ ☐

PICTURE OF THE DAY

DRAW, SKETCH OR STICK-IN A PICTURE OR KEEPSAKE OF YOUR DAY.

DATE:........................ LOCATION:... TODAY'S STAR RATING: ☆ ☆ ☆ ☆ ☆

TRAVELLED BY: ✈ PLANE ☐ 🚢 BOAT ☐ 🛣 ROAD ☐ 🪧 WALK ☐ 🎈 OTHER ☐

WHERE DID I VISIT?

WHO WAS THERE?

WHAT I DISCOVERED?

WHO DID I MEET?

MY FAVOURITE THING WAS:

MY MOOD WAS 😄 ☐ 🙂 ☐ 😐 ☐ 🙁 ☐ 😎 ☐ 😴 ☐

WEATHER ☀ ☐ ⛅ ☐ 🌦 ☐ ⛈ ☐ 🌧 ☐ 🌨 ☐

PICTURE OF THE DAY

DRAW, SKETCH OR STICK-IN A PICTURE OR KEEPSAKE OF YOUR DAY.

DATE:........................ LOCATION:....................................... TODAY'S STAR RATING: ☆☆☆☆☆

TRAVELLED BY: ✈ PLANE ☐ 🚢 BOAT ☐ 🏍 ROAD ☐ 🪧 WALK ☐ 🎈 OTHER ☐

WHERE DID I VISIT?

WHO WAS THERE?

WHAT I DISCOVERED?

WHO DID I MEET?

MY FAVOURITE THING WAS:

MY MOOD WAS 😄 ☐ 🙂 ☐ 😐 ☐ 🙁 ☐ 😎 ☐ 😴 ☐

WEATHER ☀ ☐ ⛅ ☐ 🌦 ☐ ⛈ ☐ 🌧 ☐ 🌨 ☐

PICTURE OF THE DAY

DRAW, SKETCH OR STICK-IN A PICTURE OR KEEPSAKE OF YOUR DAY.

DATE:......................... LOCATION:....................................... TODAY'S STAR RATING: ☆☆☆☆☆

TRAVELLED BY: ✈ PLANE ☐ 🚢 BOAT ☐ 🛣 ROAD ☐ 🪧 WALK ☐ 🎈 OTHER ☐

WHERE DID I VISIT?

WHO WAS THERE?

WHAT I DISCOVERED?

WHO DID I MEET?

MY FAVOURITE THING WAS:

MY MOOD WAS 😄 ☐ 🙂 ☐ 😐 ☐ 🙁 ☐ 😎 ☐ 😴 ☐

WEATHER ☀ ☐ ⛅ ☐ 🌦 ☐ ⛈ ☐ 🌧 ☐ 🌨 ☐

PICTURE OF THE DAY

DRAW, SKETCH OR STICK-IN A PICTURE OR KEEPSAKE OF YOUR DAY.

DATE:.................... LOCATION:... TODAY'S STAR RATING: ☆ ☆ ☆ ☆ ☆

TRAVELLED BY: ✈ ☐   🚢 ☐   🛣 ☐   🪧 ☐   🎈 ☐
PLANE   BOAT   ROAD   WALK   OTHER

WHERE DID I VISIT?

WHO WAS THERE?

WHAT I DISCOVERED?

WHO DID I MEET?

MY FAVOURITE THING WAS:

MY MOOD WAS   😄 ☐   🙂 ☐   😐 ☐   🙁 ☐   😎 ☐   😴 ☐

WEATHER   ☀ ☐   ⛅ ☐   🌦 ☐   ⛈ ☐   🌧 ☐   🌨 ☐

PICTURE OF THE DAY

DRAW, SKETCH OR STICK-IN A PICTURE OR KEEPSAKE OF YOUR DAY.

DATE:........................ LOCATION:... TODAY'S STAR RATING: ☆ ☆ ☆ ☆ ☆

TRAVELLED BY: ✈ □ 🚢 □ 🛣 □ 🪧 □ 🎈 □
PLANE   BOAT   ROAD   WALK   OTHER

WHERE DID I VISIT?

WHO WAS THERE?

WHAT I DISCOVERED?

WHO DID I MEET?

MY FAVOURITE THING WAS:

MY MOOD WAS 😄 □ 🙂 □ 😐 □ 🙁 □ 😎 □ 😴 □

WEATHER ☀ □ ⛅ □ 🌦 □ ⛈ □ 🌧 □ 🌨 □

PICTURE OF THE DAY

DRAW, SKETCH OR STICK-IN A PICTURE OR KEEPSAKE OF YOUR DAY.

DATE:.................... LOCATION:... TODAY'S STAR RATING: ☆☆☆☆☆

TRAVELLED BY: ✈ PLANE ☐ 🚢 BOAT ☐ 🛤 ROAD ☐ 🪧 WALK ☐ 🎈 OTHER ☐

WHERE DID I VISIT?

WHO WAS THERE?

WHAT I DISCOVERED?

WHO DID I MEET?

MY FAVOURITE THING WAS:

MY MOOD WAS 😄 ☐ 🙂 ☐ 😐 ☐ 🙁 ☐ 😎 ☐ 😴 ☐

WEATHER ☀ ☐ ⛅ ☐ 🌦 ☐ ⛈ ☐ 🌧 ☐ 🌨 ☐

PICTURE OF THE DAY

DRAW, SKETCH OR STICK-IN A PICTURE OR KEEPSAKE OF YOUR DAY.

DATE:......................... LOCATION:.. TODAY'S STAR RATING: ☆☆☆☆☆

TRAVELLED BY: ✈ ☐ 🚢 ☐ 🛣 ☐ 🪧 ☐ 🎈 ☐
PLANE   BOAT   ROAD   WALK   OTHER

WHERE DID I VISIT?

WHO WAS THERE?

WHAT I DISCOVERED?

WHO DID I MEET?

MY FAVOURITE THING WAS:

MY MOOD WAS 😆 ☐ 🙂 ☐ 😐 ☐ ☹ ☐ 😎 ☐ 😴 ☐

WEATHER ☀ ☐ ⛅ ☐ 🌦 ☐ ⛈ ☐ 🌧 ☐ 🌨 ☐

PICTURE OF THE DAY

DRAW, SKETCH OR STICK-IN A PICTURE OR KEEPSAKE OF YOUR DAY.

DATE:........................ LOCATION:.. TODAY'S STAR RATING: ☆ ☆ ☆ ☆ ☆

TRAVELLED BY: ✈ PLANE ☐ 🚢 BOAT ☐ 🛣 ROAD ☐ 🪧 WALK ☐ 🎈 OTHER ☐

WHERE DID I VISIT?

WHO WAS THERE?

WHAT I DISCOVERED?

WHO DID I MEET?

MY FAVOURITE THING WAS:

MY MOOD WAS 😄 ☐ 🙂 ☐ 😐 ☐ 🙁 ☐ 😎 ☐ 😴 ☐

WEATHER ☀ ☐ ⛅ ☐ 🌦 ☐ ⛈ ☐ 🌧 ☐ 🌨 ☐

PICTURE OF THE DAY

DRAW, SKETCH OR STICK-IN A PICTURE OR KEEPSAKE OF YOUR DAY.

DATE:........................ LOCATION:... TODAY'S STAR RATING: ☆ ☆ ☆ ☆ ☆

TRAVELLED BY: ✈ PLANE ☐ 🚢 BOAT ☐ 🛣 ROAD ☐ 🪧 WALK ☐ 🎈 OTHER ☐

WHERE DID I VISIT?

WHO WAS THERE?

WHAT I DISCOVERED?

WHO DID I MEET?

MY FAVOURITE THING WAS:

MY MOOD WAS 😆 ☐ 🙂 ☐ 😐 ☐ 🙁 ☐ 😎 ☐ 😴 ☐

WEATHER ☀ ☐ ⛅ ☐ 🌦 ☐ ⛈ ☐ 🌧 ☐ 🌨 ☐

PICTURE OF THE DAY

DRAW, SKETCH OR STICK-IN A PICTURE OR KEEPSAKE OF YOUR DAY.

DATE:.................... LOCATION:... TODAY'S STAR RATING: ☆ ☆ ☆ ☆ ☆

TRAVELLED BY: ✈ PLANE ☐ 🚢 BOAT ☐ 🛣 ROAD ☐ 🪧 WALK ☐ 🎈 OTHER ☐

WHERE DID I VISIT?

WHO WAS THERE?

WHAT I DISCOVERED?

WHO DID I MEET?

MY FAVOURITE THING WAS:

MY MOOD WAS 😄 ☐ 🙂 ☐ 😐 ☐ 🙁 ☐ 😎 ☐ 😴 ☐

WEATHER ☀ ☐ ⛅ ☐ 🌦 ☐ ⛈ ☐ 🌧 ☐ 🌨 ☐

PICTURE OF THE DAY

DRAW, SKETCH OR STICK-IN A PICTURE OR KEEPSAKE OF YOUR DAY.

DATE:........................ LOCATION:.. TODAY'S STAR RATING: ☆☆☆☆☆

TRAVELLED BY: PLANE ☐ BOAT ☐ ROAD ☐ WALK ☐ OTHER ☐

WHERE DID I VISIT?

WHO WAS THERE?

WHAT I DISCOVERED?

WHO DID I MEET?

MY FAVOURITE THING WAS:

MY MOOD WAS 😄 ☐ 🙂 ☐ 😐 ☐ 🙁 ☐ 😎 ☐ 😴 ☐

WEATHER ☀ ☐ ⛅ ☐ 🌦 ☐ ⛈ ☐ 🌧 ☐ 🌨 ☐

PICTURE OF THE DAY

DRAW, SKETCH OR STICK-IN A PICTURE OR KEEPSAKE OF YOUR DAY.

DATE:........................ LOCATION:... TODAY'S STAR RATING: ☆☆☆☆☆

TRAVELLED BY: ✈ PLANE ☐   🚢 BOAT ☐   🛣 ROAD ☐   🪧 WALK ☐   🎈 OTHER ☐

WHERE DID I VISIT?

WHO WAS THERE?

WHAT I DISCOVERED?

WHO DID I MEET?

MY FAVOURITE THING WAS:

MY MOOD WAS 😄 ☐ 🙂 ☐ 😐 ☐ 🙁 ☐ 😎 ☐ 😴 ☐

WEATHER ☀ ☐ ⛅ ☐ 🌦 ☐ ⛈ ☐ 🌧 ☐ ❄ ☐

PICTURE OF THE DAY

DRAW, SKETCH OR STICK-IN A PICTURE OR KEEPSAKE OF YOUR DAY.

DATE:........................ LOCATION:... TODAY'S STAR RATING: ☆ ☆ ☆ ☆ ☆

TRAVELLED BY: ✈ ☐ 🚢 ☐ 🛣 ☐ 🪧 ☐ 🎈 ☐
PLANE BOAT ROAD WALK OTHER

WHERE DID I VISIT?

WHO WAS THERE?

WHAT I DISCOVERED?

WHO DID I MEET?

MY FAVOURITE THING WAS:

MY MOOD WAS 😄 ☐ 🙂 ☐ 😐 ☐ 🙁 ☐ 😎 ☐ 😴 ☐

WEATHER ☀ ☐ ⛅ ☐ 🌦 ☐ ⛈ ☐ 🌧 ☐ 🌨 ☐

PICTURE OF THE DAY

DRAW, SKETCH OR STICK-IN A PICTURE OR KEEPSAKE OF YOUR DAY.

DATE:........................ LOCATION:... TODAY'S STAR RATING: ☆☆☆☆☆

TRAVELLED BY: ✈ □ 🚢 □ 🛣 □ 🪧 □ 🎈 □
PLANE BOAT ROAD WALK OTHER

WHERE DID I VISIT?

WHO WAS THERE?

WHAT I DISCOVERED?

WHO DID I MEET?

MY FAVOURITE THING WAS:

MY MOOD WAS 😄 □ 🙂 □ 😐 □ 🙁 □ 😎 □ 😴 □

WEATHER ☀ □ ⛅ □ 🌥 □ ⛈ □ 🌧 □ 🌨 □

PICTURE OF THE DAY

DRAW, SKETCH OR STICK-IN A PICTURE OR KEEPSAKE OF YOUR DAY.

DATE:........................ LOCATION:.. TODAY'S STAR RATING: ☆☆☆☆☆

TRAVELLED BY: PLANE ☐ BOAT ☐ ROAD ☐ WALK ☐ OTHER ☐

WHERE DID I VISIT?

WHO WAS THERE?

WHAT I DISCOVERED?

WHO DID I MEET?

MY FAVOURITE THING WAS:

MY MOOD WAS 😄 ☐ 🙂 ☐ 😐 ☐ 🙁 ☐ 😎 ☐ 😴 ☐

WEATHER ☀ ☐ ⛅ ☐ 🌦 ☐ ⛈ ☐ 🌧 ☐ 🌨 ☐

PICTURE OF THE DAY

DRAW, SKETCH OR STICK-IN A PICTURE OR KEEPSAKE OF YOUR DAY.

DATE:...................... LOCATION:.. TODAY'S STAR RATING: ☆ ☆ ☆ ☆ ☆

TRAVELLED BY: ✈ ☐ 🚢 ☐ 🛣 ☐ 🪧 ☐ 🎈 ☐
PLANE   BOAT   ROAD   WALK   OTHER

WHERE DID I VISIT?

WHO WAS THERE?

WHAT I DISCOVERED?

WHO DID I MEET?

MY FAVOURITE THING WAS:

MY MOOD WAS 😆 ☐ 🙂 ☐ 😐 ☐ 🙁 ☐ 😎 ☐ 😴 ☐

WEATHER ☀ ☐ ⛅ ☐ 🌦 ☐ ⛈ ☐ 🌧 ☐ 🌨 ☐

PICTURE OF THE DAY

DRAW, SKETCH OR STICK-IN A PICTURE OR KEEPSAKE OF YOUR DAY.

DATE:........................ LOCATION:.. TODAY'S STAR RATING: ☆☆☆☆☆

TRAVELLED BY: ✈ PLANE ☐ 🚢 BOAT ☐ 🛣 ROAD ☐ 🪧 WALK ☐ 🎈 OTHER ☐

WHERE DID I VISIT?

WHO WAS THERE?

WHAT I DISCOVERED?

WHO DID I MEET?

MY FAVOURITE THING WAS:

MY MOOD WAS 😄 ☐ 🙂 ☐ 😐 ☐ 🙁 ☐ 😎 ☐ 😴 ☐

WEATHER ☀ ☐ ⛅ ☐ 🌦 ☐ ⛈ ☐ 🌧 ☐ 🌨 ☐

PICTURE OF THE DAY

DRAW, SKETCH OR STICK-IN A PICTURE OR KEEPSAKE OF YOUR DAY.

DATE:........................ LOCATION:... TODAY'S STAR RATING: ☆☆☆☆☆

TRAVELLED BY: ✈ □ PLANE 🚢 □ BOAT 🛣 □ ROAD 🪧 □ WALK 🎈 □ OTHER

WHERE DID I VISIT?

WHO WAS THERE?

WHAT I DISCOVERED?

WHO DID I MEET?

MY FAVOURITE THING WAS:

MY MOOD WAS 😄 □ 🙂 □ 😐 □ 🙁 □ 😎 □ 😴 □

WEATHER ☀ □ ⛅ □ 🌦 □ ⛈ □ 🌧 □ 🌨 □

PICTURE OF THE DAY

DRAW, SKETCH OR STICK-IN A PICTURE OR KEEPSAKE OF YOUR DAY.

DATE:........................ LOCATION:.. TODAY'S STAR RATING: ☆☆☆☆☆

TRAVELLED BY: PLANE ☐ BOAT ☐ ROAD ☐ WALK ☐ OTHER ☐

WHERE DID I VISIT?

WHO WAS THERE?

WHAT I DISCOVERED?

WHO DID I MEET?

MY FAVOURITE THING WAS:

MY MOOD WAS 😄 ☐ 🙂 ☐ 😐 ☐ 🙁 ☐ 😎 ☐ 😴 ☐

WEATHER ☀ ☐ ⛅ ☐ 🌦 ☐ ⛈ ☐ 🌧 ☐ 🌨 ☐

PICTURE OF THE DAY

DRAW, SKETCH OR STICK-IN A PICTURE OR KEEPSAKE OF YOUR DAY.

DATE:................ LOCATION:................................... TODAY'S STAR RATING: ☆ ☆ ☆ ☆ ☆

TRAVELLED BY: ✈ □ 🚢 □ 🚗 □ 🪧 □ 🎈 □
             PLANE   BOAT   ROAD   WALK   OTHER

WHERE DID I VISIT?

WHO WAS THERE?

WHAT I DISCOVERED?

WHO DID I MEET?

MY FAVOURITE THING WAS:

MY MOOD WAS 😄 □ 🙂 □ 😐 □ 🙁 □ 😎 □ 😴 □

WEATHER ☀ □ ⛅ □ 🌦 □ ⛈ □ 🌧 □ 🌨 □

PICTURE OF THE DAY

DRAW, SKETCH OR STICK-IN A PICTURE OR KEEPSAKE OF YOUR DAY.

DATE:........................ LOCATION:.. TODAY'S STAR RATING: ☆ ☆ ☆ ☆ ☆

TRAVELLED BY: ✈ PLANE ☐ 🚢 BOAT ☐ 🛤 ROAD ☐ 🪧 WALK ☐ 🎈 OTHER ☐

WHERE DID I VISIT?

WHO WAS THERE?

WHAT I DISCOVERED?

WHO DID I MEET?

MY FAVOURITE THING WAS:

MY MOOD WAS 😄 ☐ 🙂 ☐ 😐 ☐ ☹ ☐ 😎 ☐ 😴 ☐

WEATHER ☀ ☐ ⛅ ☐ 🌦 ☐ ⛈ ☐ 🌧 ☐ 🌨 ☐

PICTURE OF THE DAY

DRAW, SKETCH OR STICK-IN A PICTURE OR KEEPSAKE OF YOUR DAY.

DATE:.......................... LOCATION:... TODAY'S STAR RATING: ☆ ☆ ☆ ☆ ☆

TRAVELLED BY:
PLANE ☐ BOAT ☐ ROAD ☐ WALK ☐ OTHER ☐

WHERE DID I VISIT?

WHO WAS THERE?

WHAT I DISCOVERED?

WHO DID I MEET?

MY FAVOURITE THING WAS:

MY MOOD WAS ☺ ☐ ☺ ☐ ☺ ☐ ☹ ☐ 😎 ☐ 😴 ☐

WEATHER ☀ ☐ ⛅ ☐ 🌦 ☐ ⛈ ☐ 🌧 ☐ ❄ ☐

PICTURE OF THE DAY

DRAW, SKETCH OR STICK-IN A PICTURE OR KEEPSAKE OF YOUR DAY.

DATE:.................... LOCATION:... TODAY'S STAR RATING: ☆☆☆☆☆

TRAVELLED BY: ✈ PLANE ☐ 🚢 BOAT ☐ 🛣 ROAD ☐ 🪧 WALK ☐ 🎈 OTHER ☐

WHERE DID I VISIT?

WHO WAS THERE?

WHAT I DISCOVERED?

WHO DID I MEET?

MY FAVOURITE THING WAS:

MY MOOD WAS 😄 ☐ 🙂 ☐ 😐 ☐ 🙁 ☐ 😎 ☐ 😴 ☐

WEATHER ☀ ☐ ⛅ ☐ 🌦 ☐ ⛈ ☐ 🌧 ☐ 🌨 ☐

PICTURE OF THE DAY

DRAW, SKETCH OR STICK-IN A PICTURE OR KEEPSAKE OF YOUR DAY.

DATE:.................... LOCATION:.. TODAY'S STAR RATING: ☆ ☆ ☆ ☆ ☆

TRAVELLED BY: ✈ □ 🚢 □ 🛣 □ 🪧 □ 🎈 □
             PLANE   BOAT   ROAD   WALK   OTHER

WHERE DID I VISIT?

WHO WAS THERE?

WHAT I DISCOVERED?

WHO DID I MEET?

MY FAVOURITE THING WAS:

MY MOOD WAS 😄 □ 🙂 □ 😐 □ 🙁 □ 😎 □ 😴 □

WEATHER ☀ □ ⛅ □ 🌦 □ ⛈ □ 🌧 □ 🌨 □

PICTURE OF THE DAY

DRAW, SKETCH OR STICK-IN A PICTURE OR KEEPSAKE OF YOUR DAY.

DATE:.................... LOCATION:.. TODAY'S STAR RATING: ☆ ☆ ☆ ☆ ☆

TRAVELLED BY: PLANE ☐ BOAT ☐ ROAD ☐ WALK ☐ OTHER ☐

WHERE DID I VISIT?

WHO WAS THERE?

WHAT I DISCOVERED?

WHO DID I MEET?

MY FAVOURITE THING WAS:

MY MOOD WAS 😄 ☐ 🙂 ☐ 😐 ☐ 🙁 ☐ 😎 ☐ 😴 ☐

WEATHER ☀ ☐ ⛅ ☐ 🌦 ☐ ⛈ ☐ 🌧 ☐ ❄ ☐

PICTURE OF THE DAY

DRAW, SKETCH OR STICK-IN A PICTURE OR KEEPSAKE OF YOUR DAY.

DATE:........................ LOCATION:.. TODAY'S STAR RATING: ☆ ☆ ☆ ☆ ☆

TRAVELLED BY: ✈ ☐ 🚢 ☐ 🛣 ☐ 🪧 ☐ 🎈 ☐
PLANE   BOAT   ROAD   WALK   OTHER

WHERE DID I VISIT?

WHO WAS THERE?

WHAT I DISCOVERED?

WHO DID I MEET?

MY FAVOURITE THING WAS:

MY MOOD WAS 😄 ☐ 🙂 ☐ 😐 ☐ 🙁 ☐ 😎 ☐ 😴 ☐

WEATHER ☀ ☐ ⛅ ☐ 🌦 ☐ ⛈ ☐ 🌧 ☐ 🌨 ☐

PICTURE OF THE DAY

DRAW, SKETCH OR STICK-IN A PICTURE OR KEEPSAKE OF YOUR DAY.

DATE: .... LOCATION: .... TODAY'S STAR RATING: ☆ ☆ ☆ ☆ ☆

TRAVELLED BY: ✈ □ 🚢 □ 🛣 □ 🪧 □ 🎈 □
PLANE   BOAT   ROAD   WALK   OTHER

WHERE DID I VISIT?

WHO WAS THERE?

WHAT I DISCOVERED?

WHO DID I MEET?

MY FAVOURITE THING WAS:

MY MOOD WAS 😄 □ 🙂 □ 😐 □ 🙁 □ 😎 □ 😴 □

WEATHER ☀ □ ⛅ □ 🌦 □ ⛈ □ 🌧 □ 🌨 □

PICTURE OF THE DAY

DRAW, SKETCH OR STICK-IN A PICTURE OR KEEPSAKE OF YOUR DAY.

DATE:..................... LOCATION:... TODAY'S STAR RATING: ☆☆☆☆☆

TRAVELLED BY: ✈ PLANE ☐ 🚢 BOAT ☐ 🛣 ROAD ☐ 🪧 WALK ☐ 🎈 OTHER ☐

WHERE DID I VISIT?

WHO WAS THERE?

WHAT I DISCOVERED?

WHO DID I MEET?

MY FAVOURITE THING WAS:

MY MOOD WAS 😄 ☐ 🙂 ☐ 😐 ☐ 🙁 ☐ 😎 ☐ 😴 ☐

WEATHER ☀ ☐ ⛅ ☐ 🌦 ☐ ⛈ ☐ 🌧 ☐ 🌨 ☐

PICTURE OF THE DAY

DRAW, SKETCH OR STICK-IN A PICTURE OR KEEPSAKE OF YOUR DAY.

DATE:........................ LOCATION:... TODAY'S STAR RATING: ☆☆☆☆☆

TRAVELLED BY: ✈ □ 🚢 □ 🛣 □ 🪧 □ 🎈 □
PLANE   BOAT   ROAD   WALK   OTHER

WHERE DID I VISIT?

WHO WAS THERE?

WHAT I DISCOVERED?

WHO DID I MEET?

MY FAVOURITE THING WAS:

MY MOOD WAS 😄 □ 🙂 □ 😐 □ 🙁 □ 😎 □ 😴 □

WEATHER ☀ □ ⛅ □ 🌦 □ ⛈ □ ☁ □ 🌨 □

PICTURE OF THE DAY

DRAW, SKETCH OR STICK-IN A PICTURE OR KEEPSAKE OF YOUR DAY.

DATE:........................ LOCATION:... TODAY'S STAR RATING: ☆☆☆☆☆

TRAVELLED BY: ✈ ☐ 🚢 ☐ 🛣 ☐ 🪧 ☐ 🎈 ☐
PLANE   BOAT   ROAD   WALK   OTHER

WHERE DID I VISIT?

WHO WAS THERE?

WHAT I DISCOVERED?

WHO DID I MEET?

MY FAVOURITE THING WAS:

MY MOOD WAS 😄 ☐ 🙂 ☐ 😐 ☐ 🙁 ☐ 😎 ☐ 😴 ☐

WEATHER ☀ ☐ ⛅ ☐ 🌦 ☐ ⛈ ☐ 🌧 ☐ 🌨 ☐

PICTURE OF THE DAY

DRAW, SKETCH OR STICK-IN A PICTURE OR KEEPSAKE OF YOUR DAY.

DATE:........................ LOCATION:.. TODAY'S STAR RATING: ☆☆☆☆☆

TRAVELLED BY:
PLANE ☐ BOAT ☐ ROAD ☐ WALK ☐ OTHER ☐

WHERE DID I VISIT?

WHO WAS THERE?

WHAT I DISCOVERED?

WHO DID I MEET?

MY FAVOURITE THING WAS:

MY MOOD WAS ☐ ☐ ☐ ☐ ☐ ☐

WEATHER ☐ ☐ ☐ ☐ ☐ ☐

PICTURE OF THE DAY

DRAW, SKETCH OR STICK-IN A PICTURE OR KEEPSAKE OF YOUR DAY.

DATE:.................... LOCATION:.. TODAY'S STAR RATING: ☆ ☆ ☆ ☆ ☆

TRAVELLED BY: ✈ PLANE ☐ 🚢 BOAT ☐ 🛣 ROAD ☐ 🪧 WALK ☐ 🎈 OTHER ☐

WHERE DID I VISIT?

WHO WAS THERE?

WHAT I DISCOVERED?

WHO DID I MEET?

MY FAVOURITE THING WAS:

MY MOOD WAS 😄 ☐ 🙂 ☐ 😐 ☐ ☹ ☐ 😎 ☐ 😴 ☐

WEATHER ☀ ☐ ⛅ ☐ 🌦 ☐ ⛈ ☐ 🌧 ☐ 🌨 ☐

PICTURE OF THE DAY

DRAW, SKETCH OR STICK-IN A PICTURE OR KEEPSAKE OF YOUR DAY.

DATE:........................ LOCATION: .... TODAY'S STAR RATING: ☆ ☆ ☆ ☆ ☆

TRAVELLED BY: ✈ □ 🚢 □ 🛣 □ 🪧 □ 🎈 □
               PLANE   BOAT   ROAD   WALK   OTHER

WHERE DID I VISIT?
📍

WHO WAS THERE?

WHAT I DISCOVERED?

WHO DID I MEET?

MY FAVOURITE THING WAS:

MY MOOD WAS 😆 □ 🙂 □ 😐 □ ☹ □ 😎 □ 😴 □

WEATHER ☀ □ ⛅ □ 🌦 □ ⛈ □ ☁ □ 🌨 □

PICTURE OF THE DAY

DRAW, SKETCH OR STICK-IN A PICTURE OR KEEPSAKE OF YOUR DAY.

DATE:........................ LOCATION: .... TODAY'S STAR RATING: ☆ ☆ ☆ ☆ ☆

TRAVELLED BY: ✈ ☐   🚢 ☐   🛣 ☐   🪧 ☐   🎈 ☐
PLANE   BOAT   ROAD   WALK   OTHER

WHERE DID I VISIT?

WHO WAS THERE?

WHAT I DISCOVERED?

WHO DID I MEET?

MY FAVOURITE THING WAS:

MY MOOD WAS 😄 ☐ 🙂 ☐ 😐 ☐ 🙁 ☐ 😎 ☐ 😴 ☐

WEATHER ☀ ☐ ⛅ ☐ 🌦 ☐ ⛈ ☐ 🌧 ☐ 🌨 ☐

PICTURE OF THE DAY

DRAW, SKETCH OR STICK-IN A PICTURE OR KEEPSAKE OF YOUR DAY.

DATE:........................ LOCATION:... TODAY'S STAR RATING: ☆☆☆☆☆

TRAVELLED BY: 🛩 ☐ 🚢 ☐ 🛤 ☐ 🪧 ☐ 🎈 ☐
PLANE   BOAT   ROAD   WALK   OTHER

WHERE DID I VISIT?

WHO WAS THERE?

WHAT I DISCOVERED?

WHO DID I MEET?

MY FAVOURITE THING WAS:

MY MOOD WAS 😆 ☐ 🙂 ☐ 😐 ☐ 🙁 ☐ 😎 ☐ 😴 ☐

WEATHER ☀ ☐ ⛅ ☐ 🌦 ☐ ⛈ ☐ 🌧 ☐ ❄ ☐

PICTURE OF THE DAY

DRAW, SKETCH OR STICK-IN A PICTURE OR KEEPSAKE OF YOUR DAY.

DATE:......................... LOCATION:.. TODAY'S STAR RATING: ☆ ☆ ☆ ☆ ☆

TRAVELLED BY: ✈ ☐ 🚢 ☐ 🛣 ☐ 🪧 ☐ 🎈 ☐
PLANE   BOAT   ROAD   WALK   OTHER

WHERE DID I VISIT?

WHO WAS THERE?

WHAT I DISCOVERED?

WHO DID I MEET?

MY FAVOURITE THING WAS:

MY MOOD WAS 😄 ☐ 🙂 ☐ 😐 ☐ 🙁 ☐ 😎 ☐ 😴 ☐

WEATHER ☀ ☐ ⛅ ☐ 🌦 ☐ ⛈ ☐ 🌧 ☐ ❄ ☐

PICTURE OF THE DAY

DRAW, SKETCH OR STICK-IN A PICTURE OR KEEPSAKE OF YOUR DAY.

DATE:.......................... LOCATION:... TODAY'S STAR RATING: ☆☆☆☆☆

TRAVELLED BY: ✈ PLANE ☐ 🚢 BOAT ☐ 🛣 ROAD ☐ 🪧 WALK ☐ 🎈 OTHER ☐

WHERE DID I VISIT?

WHO WAS THERE?

WHAT I DISCOVERED?

WHO DID I MEET?

MY FAVOURITE THING WAS:

MY MOOD WAS 😄 ☐ 🙂 ☐ 😐 ☐ 🙁 ☐ 😎 ☐ 😴 ☐

WEATHER ☀ ☐ ⛅ ☐ 🌥 ☐ ⛈ ☐ 🌧 ☐ 🌨 ☐

PICTURE OF THE DAY

DRAW, SKETCH OR STICK-IN A PICTURE OR KEEPSAKE OF YOUR DAY.

DATE:................. LOCATION:................................. TODAY'S STAR RATING: ☆☆☆☆☆

TRAVELLED BY: ✈ PLANE ☐ 🚢 BOAT ☐ 🚗 ROAD ☐ 🪧 WALK ☐ 🎈 OTHER ☐

WHERE DID I VISIT?

WHO WAS THERE?

WHAT I DISCOVERED?

WHO DID I MEET?

MY FAVOURITE THING WAS:

MY MOOD WAS 😄☐ 🙂☐ 😐☐ ☹️☐ 😎☐ 😴☐

WEATHER ☀️☐ ⛅☐ 🌤️☐ ⛈️☐ 🌧️☐ 🌨️☐

PICTURE OF THE DAY

DRAW, SKETCH OR STICK-IN A PICTURE OR KEEPSAKE OF YOUR DAY.

DATE:...................... LOCATION:.. TODAY'S STAR RATING: ☆ ☆ ☆ ☆ ☆

TRAVELLED BY: ✈ PLANE ☐ 🚢 BOAT ☐ 🛣 ROAD ☐ 🪧 WALK ☐ 🎈 OTHER ☐

WHERE DID I VISIT?

WHO WAS THERE?

WHAT I DISCOVERED?

WHO DID I MEET?

MY FAVOURITE THING WAS:

MY MOOD WAS 😄 ☐ 🙂 ☐ 😐 ☐ ☹ ☐ 😎 ☐ 😴 ☐

WEATHER ☀ ☐ ⛅ ☐ 🌦 ☐ ⛈ ☐ 🌧 ☐ 🌨 ☐

PICTURE OF THE DAY

DRAW, SKETCH OR STICK-IN A PICTURE OR KEEPSAKE OF YOUR DAY.

DATE:........................ LOCATION:.. TODAY'S STAR RATING: ☆ ☆ ☆ ☆ ☆

TRAVELLED BY: ✈ ☐ 🚢 ☐ 🚗 ☐ 🪧 ☐ 🎈 ☐
PLANE   BOAT   ROAD   WALK   OTHER

WHERE DID I VISIT?

WHO WAS THERE?

WHAT I DISCOVERED?

WHO DID I MEET?

MY FAVOURITE THING WAS:

MY MOOD WAS 😄 ☐ 🙂 ☐ 😐 ☐ 🙁 ☐ 😎 ☐ 😴 ☐

WEATHER ☀ ☐ ⛅ ☐ 🌥 ☐ ⛈ ☐ 🌧 ☐ 🌨 ☐

PICTURE OF THE DAY

DRAW, SKETCH OR STICK-IN A PICTURE OR KEEPSAKE OF YOUR DAY.

THE BEST
TRIP

Made in the USA
Monee, IL
11 July 2022

99508227R00057